Tethered

to

Stars

ALSO BY FADY JOUDAH

Tethered

to

Stars

poems

FADY JOUDAH

MILKWEED EDITIONS

Published 2021 by Milkweed Editions
Printed in Canada
Cover design by Mary Austin Speaker
Cover art by Gervasio Troche
21 22 23 24 25   5 4 3 2
First Edition

Milkweed Editions, an independent nonprofit publisher, gratefully acknowledges sustaining support from our Board of Directors; the Alan B. Slifka Foundation and its president, Riva Ariella Ritvo-Slifka; the Amazon Literary Partnership; the Ballard Spahr Foundation; *Copper Nickel*; the McKnight Foundation; the National Endowment for the Arts; the National Poetry Series; the Target Foundation; and other generous contributions from foundations, corporations, and individuals. Also, this activity is made possible by the voters of Minnesota through a Minnesota State Arts Board Operating Support grant, thanks to a legislative appropriation from the arts and cultural heritage fund. For a full listing of Milkweed Editions supporters, please visit milkweed.org.

Library of Congress Cataloging-in-Publication Data

Names: Joudah, Fady, 1971- author.
Title: Tethered to stars : poems / Fady Joudah.
Description: First Edition. | Minneapolis, Minnesota : Milkweed Editions, [2021] | Summary: "From Fady Joudah, an elegant collection of poems that shifts deftly between the microscope, the telescope, and the horoscope"-- Provided by publisher.
Identifiers: LCCN 2020038692 (print) | LCCN 2020038693 (ebook) | ISBN 9781571315342 (paperback) | ISBN 9781571317315 (ebook)
Subjects: LCGFT: Poetry.
Classification: LCC PS3610.O679 T45 2021 (print) | LCC PS3610.O679 (ebook) | DDC 811/.6--dc23
LC record available at https://lccn.loc.gov/2020038692
LC ebook record available at https://lccn.loc.gov/2020038693

Milkweed Editions is committed to ecological stewardship. We strive to align our book production practices with this principle and to reduce the impact of our operations in the environment. We are a member of the Green Press Initiative, a nonprofit coalition of publishers, manufacturers, and authors working to protect the world's endangered forests and conserve natural resources. *Tethered to Stars* was printed on acid-free 100% postconsumer-waste paper by Friesens Corporation.

For M, Z, & H.

Contents

A night like sea waves drapes   me with all sorts of trouble.
A night whose stars are tethered   to solid stone with linen ropes.

IMRU' AL-QAIS (6TH CENTURY A.D)

Canopus

Be an owl,
not even a sunflower

turns its head
270 degrees,

but may the need to ask me
about my darkness

never command you.
Be a sunflower,

grow old to face east,
warm in the morning,

kind to insects and bees,
and may our overlap

be two: light and light
in mouths that vary

the ninety-nine
names for snow.

Taurus

Comparing miseries   isn't a road to happiness,
and as things stand, I'm ready
          to distract my Lazarus,

whatever catatonia   or narcolepsy plays him
          dead. Return
is a dish best served as stealth—we're not birds

but we can catch ourselves on trees, or
          if I ask as a dog
I ask openly for love.   Write it: what's there to lose?

Out in the world we're with others in it
          and representation is addiction
to the blues we want   to eradicate but then

lichens us to boulders.   What is the wavelength
of euphoria?   What slit diffracts praise?

And if I walk away from you   is it   from the edge
of a shallow lake?   Did I   from the cage
          of those who can't   lung my words

unless in the shadow   of a stranger tongue?
          We're not birds   but light

after sound, maybe chimera   or hermaphrodite, sound
after light.   Last week a Chinese oracle told me

our health will suffer   precipitous decline
before we age well.

Leo

Do you think we'll ever get butterflies to lay eggs
        in our backyard after what I did to the caterpillars
        on the lemon tree?

I think you inhaled some of the larva on that tree
        and they got to your head.

Or my gut. They matured, migrated up
        my esophagus, slid down into my lungs, secreting a cough
        reflex suppressant as the worms hung upside down
        like bats, my alveoli their makeshift cocoons.

You'd better extract that cough syrup soon,
        it'll be a sensation over-the-counter.

The newly formed butterflies would gently ride my exhalations
        but not all would survive the exodus.

You probably wouldn't either. Your chest might explode
        or you might implode with asphyxiation.

Maybe. And maybe the butterflies are vested
        in preserving their host.

You'd like that, wouldn't you? Whenever you open your mouth
        a butterfly enchants us.

The Holy Embraces the Holy

1.

That you have nothing to say,
your deep sadness reserves me
as a den reserves a security blanket.

That in the mirror I see you.
You were not there.
Your silence was a mask.
I read from it.

2.

The studies done so far
have not been good studies. We agree:
more research is needed, more money allocated,
so that we practice what we return to when we say,
don't judge me. I took LSD once.

I experienced no visual or auditory hallucinations.
The drop possibly had no drop in it.
Or maybe the vendor thought to protect my friend
a young medical doctor then, from herself.
Or she overpaid. Or the hit was a gift.

3.

We went hiking. There was a rattlesnake
and I heard what it had to say.
April snow was melting in Zion National Park,
we had no wet or dry suites. I saw two currents meet,
one held off the other: at the interface
a mirror. God's face in slo-mo plumes
of dirt and gravel. Then in a self-contained

area blinded by a bluff we came across
a woman calling out to "Bob."
He was her husband, she said.
She could have been Japanese,
had an accent as I have an accent
with certain names. We offered her a few discerning
glances into the woods before my friend whispered
one of Zeno's paradoxes to me:
which story did we want to see
through on acid?

4.

Six months later in Paracas, with the same friend,
before I became the son of the mother who loved me
or loved me not, we visited the national park on the Pacific.
The resort was where stone desert is alive with sea
and no greenery negotiated life. Mindfully we went about
acquiring more debt: dinner was included,
but we didn't have enough for lunch or breakfast.
Complimentary tea or coffee with warm bread

and rolls of salted butter was what the Queen said we could eat.
By the third morning, we went for the gratis like it was a jugular.

5.

That your sadness was a silence
and your silence no mask.
That you have become epic,
no chronology sustains you.

6.

In Paracas I shroomed. No hallucination.
My grip on reality was wicked. The waves
delivered the gust to shore and I summoned
my magic carpet, straddled it like a bike,
my tiptoes on the ground. On the cliffs a fleet
of red condors pulled out their panopticons for the seals
a hundred meters below. The wind was an exalted rubble
off the edge. With their wingspan some condors rose
as if free falling then floated above waiting.

7.

Condor Legion: the air
squadron that bombed Guernica.

Historians: when they are
"camp followers" of empire.
Poets: when empire's tragic clowns.

8.

For dinner, freshly caught large sea bass
worthy of display for the dining room guests.
We did not tip the waiters, we were not yet
the great doctors of America. The driver,
we tipped. He played our kind of music
on the car radio and took us to a cave
where water cymbals crashed into stone,
and nearby fishermen pitched their rods
along the shore like streetlights.

9.

That you have nothing to say.
That your deep sadness is free
to be deeply sad near me,
some of what love is for.

10.

The week before, we'd been on the Inca trail to Machu Picchu.
The stuff about altitude sickness is real,
but so is the stuff about coca leaves.
We ascended into mist then frigid rain.
After long rain a full moon
made love to snowcapped mountains
in a cloudless sky.

11.

In the Sacred City, I wanted to visit the moon
temple on Huayna Picchu. Time said I had to take the hill
running and hopping
at a comfortable nonstop pace
so that I might make the last bus down
to Aguas Calientes. On my way up I passed
a depleted man sitting on a rock.
His half-life was visible in a plastic water bottle.
On my descent, he was near the top,
a decaying wolf who couldn't blow a house down.
I stopped to water time.

He gulped, said he was French,
asked me where I was from.

12.

Did he say "French," or did I
infer it from the few words he muttered
in his deep state of rapid heartbeat
and mediocre oxygen exchange?

He asked me first: after I insisted
he'd take an extra gulp from my canteen,
for heart and lungs to turn serene.
I took his question to mean
that he wanted to credit my kindness to a place
when he gets to tell his story.
I gave the credit to Palestine.

13.

His face, which had been a theatre of struggle,
went blank. Suddenly he was playing poker
alone. Did I have a face? Could I have passed
for several options, Algerian, Spanish, or could I
have been an Afrikaner?

Maybe "Palestine" was the last thing he expected to hear.
Or his face had nothing to do with the word.
Maybe he anticipated "American" first and foremost
because I did say "water."

14.

That in the mirror I pulled up your hands.
A pose you've shadowed
all your life isn't always a pose.

That your hands were all water,
all night, light was with us
stabbing us in the back.

15.

Years passed for years. Into a patient's room
I introduced myself with an apology.

For two weeks he'd been a hopeful captive
subjected to the merry-go-round of doctors.
A dying man with another dead person's heart
that gave him all it could.

In this world, a person is rarely transplanted
more than once. "Yes,"
was the transplanted man's response,
"you guys are like clowns in a van."

Faceless (as, in fairness,
he was to me) I burst out laughing.

16.

A few days and he mentioned endings,
said that a chaplain randomly assigned to his floor
asked him if he wanted to speak about faith.
The chaplain was Muslim, Ali,

and the patient was not that kind of Texan.
"If only more Muslims were this nice,
the world would be a better place,"
the transplanted lone-star said to me.

Leaning against the wall, hands behind my back,
I nodded in cold agreement.

17.

"You're a, a ..." he asked. I nodded yes,
neither one of us uttering the word.
"And you have a sense of humor, too.
The other day you laughed at my joke."

He loved sailing.

18.

That you have nothing to say.
From the unrequited to the unconditional

to the imaginary. That your sadness
unbuttons my heart, kneads its clowns.

That a heart remains a heart in its beyond.

Pisces

A butterfly on a filament tethered to a star:
in which direction

did the beginning move—attached
to embryonic knob
on the egg that persisted in chrysalis,

or did the string rise out
of the dorsal body,

send a message of presence
home to parent or ancestor?
Our naked eye,
all its accessories

and pixilated gadgets
can't discern the string,
can only picture it:

the near weightlessness
of her translucent scalar
wings, leaking air,
she's hitched to movement

as we are. And as ours is,
hers is never a straight line
on the lucid path

in a membranous universe.
The starry filament
is stronger than wind

which calls to her
and she's between two minds:
one that surrenders to return

and another to resist its vehicle.
We're in awe of her

wasted effort,
her entropy's purpose
as she thrashes
proximal to earth

where her alleged birth
was spotted.

      Faraway in the stars
      a kind spider
      captains her sails

while here on our planet,
each time she flutters
we say a cosmos
is insufflating
graphs.

When she joins her swarm
she's not what she was before.
Like the simurgh,

the one makes room
for the whole.

Every Hour Has an Animal

What is secret is in form: a groove
my body makes inside my head jam—no,

not the homunculus that sulcal
cortex around the threshold,
   what some call rapture
   or echo's partisan to.

   I am when I am
an almond blossom, a flower
doesn't kill another bloom.

Among the few that do
   release their toxins,
the wind does not discriminate.

A secret's only secret is its form.
And the wretched importers
   of the sublime
   can say what we haven't

of the ages we've transformed
   between ingenious diction
   and indigenous street—songs

   that look for their slippers
   on the morning after: empty

tear gas grenade for hollow

mortar shell, each
a home garden receptacle.

      Mint for basil,
      jasmine for fennel,
      lotus for cranesbill.

And a helmet for a ladle,
a linden for a maple,
a buffalo for a gazelle.

Problems of Moon Language

The debate is unbearable.
Empire warps the soul for show.
The body, we know, is torn to shreds

or smoothed into orbit. Termites, too,
abandon hill to seize new ground.
The debate is unwatchable.
Our detritus is diamond dirt. Termites,

we eat our books alive
and in metamorphosis don't end
in butterflies unless, as a mystic said,

butterflies dream of us
inside their sleep.
Our satellites are fertile,

robust and high,
for trees and monuments,

gazebos and stupas,
arks, sentinels,
and minarets.

*

The debate is unbearable.
Empire the soul for show.

The body, we know, is pulled into orbit.
Termites, too, abandon hill

to seize new ground.
The debate is unwatchable.

Our diamond dirt. Termites,
we eat our books alive

unless, as a mystic said,
arcs and minarets.

*

The debate's intolerable.
The soul in orbit.

Termites also dream
of butterflies

and minarets.

Sandra Bland, Texas

On the highway home last night
you reappeared to me opposite where I was headed,
so tell me, was it

a cigarette that bothered your jailer so?
(They let me go the one time I blew smoke
into a trooper's face.) In the footage

your final revolt. I stood before you
more than once, more than sex
and color separated us, and why
should you call a doctor kin. Sandra Bland,

we broke you down,
I say your name, how broke. You died
on the day the Hollywood sign

was dedicated. For you I name
this town, and after every woman
the police killed, a town.

*

Dear Sandra,
I just got done with hours
of Civil War documentaries. "Useless,
useless," John Wilkes Booth said
of his hands as his final words. An echo
of Kurtz's "horror." The Civil War
set a standard for modern wars,
one century into another.

And as the Confederate commander
of Andersonville prison camp felt the noose
around his neck, he, too, said
he was merely obeying orders.

Armies said. The police said.
The doctor, triaging collaterals, said.
The historian wanting us to be the greatest
said. The Civil War is a pointer to
future liberation for all kinds of folk, a milestone
in which no clear victor emerges,
since time is the master to whom
even literature submits.

*

We have schools,
counties, forts, clinics,
and at one point a hospital
named after Jefferson
Davis in Texas.
We have nothing
named after you.
Will you excuse me
for naming a poem
an imaginary place that,
as with any home,
one doesn't inhabit
all alone, even if
in a coffin one is
all that there is?
And one, not even,
and one, far more.

*

Which "we" is it I speak of? Those of us
who didn't play a part in your disintegration know
that we play a part. Not all players even
the field. We're a catalog that goes on like hypha.

If it is resuscitation I seek
through your citation

it isn't resuscitation I seek. Your mother called you
Sandy and with countless others loved your smile
beyond my arithmetic of commemoration.
Sioux City, Tucson, Tuskegee, Seattle.

*

To persuade me that war is retribution
for unspeakable sins, a comeuppance, a bit
theological for me all this. But to think
of war as entropy's work, order
and disorder in a waltz that sees
not the identities we historicize into chains
of absolute ghosts? How is it that
women (to mention one example) have
suffered greater injustice, endured
more pain than men have, what entropy is this
that singles out?

*

History has rendered this kind of math incalculable.
History manufactured out of and against our biology,
seduced as a dog is lured with a treat.
Between nuance and essentialization I sing myself.
Between cost-benefit ratio and the unattainable
I see freedom in amendments I further amend.
Between my trauma and another's passage,
speaking and the spoken for.

*

It's clear you're my pretext, Sandra, you were
an Aquarius (my dad is as well), but do zodiacs exist

for birth into the afterlife? If so, then on the date
your breath no longer tethered your body, you became
a Cancer, proliferative, this nation's sign.

*

Under that sign, ten years before your murder,
I asked myself in Darfur, what is the threshold
for suffering to create us equal? It's low

enough for anyone to dance the limbo
and stay on their feet the whole
song through if we choose. I fear our twin
consciousness cannot hold. Our voodoo

and epigenetics, our quantum and wizards,
snakes and ladders. Yet my weakest faith
(when I remember it) is that I don't visit
my grief upon those whose pain is more acute

than mine, or is chronic with more frequent flares.
Is there an equation to help me exempt
others from my loyalty oath to taxonomy,
a step in my deliverance from woe?

*

Nuance, too, competes with generality
for erasure, a visibility each mode can perform

well: where is that threshold?
So that prudent justice isn't laundered

against the baler angels of our nature, Sandra,
I rise up from my apoptosis under

a cherry tree into an olive. What crimes
won't I pardon or dissipate into energy

if suffering is folded in space-time?
Is our empathy's nebula pacifist

or a ruse of the tongue sat in dentition?
I reckon the ten words in which Honest Abe

counted "the people" a trinity at Gettysburg
are what the Black Panthers heard.

*

Ms. Bland,
I also learned
that singularity
is achieved only
when one is torn
to irreconcilable
pieces, decomposed
six fathoms up,
down, lateral,
unflagged, indivisible,
undertow for all.

Ms. Bland,
how much
of me is you
and you is we?

Neon

We rock bottom,
we simulacrum,
we nothing but air,
we divan.

We Styrofoam,
we fashion spume,
Om and Ohm,
we divan.

We pyramid eat,
we worship sweet,
we belly kiss

and dimple hips,
jinn and wine,
we divan.

Listening Suture

A beam of photons, muons,
say 17.3% are remnants of the deceased
or, in planetary demographics,
       it's 71.3%—I can't say
       whose dead, if any are mine
or had journeyed from other galaxies
on home or away legs, they're here,
riding it out on beach nimbus monarchs
       as if light never ends.

A silver dolphin then two
glisten black, arch their spines as pelicans
play eureka with leaping argent fish.
       I'm with my family,
       encore, liquid or flesh,
       displacement is a body.

"There's no center that isn't made up
       of periphery," my daughter says,
the two of us knee-deep in Gulf water
whose clarity is Mississippi silt. I say,
       "And within each periphery
       a center rises up." On the drive back

lightning struck summer's habit.
She was at the wheel
       and hard rain pounded the highway,
the windshield's lids too slow for the din.
       Her knuckles turned pale.
       "Here comes an underpass," I said.
       "A series of them," she said.

Dehiscence

I didn't say goodbye to the kids.
I knelt into my weeping until my heart broke me awake.
My forehead touched the floor.
If dream is memory, I was captured in a van,
incarcerated. I was and wasn't a leader. The prison
was a camp in the wilderness. Its warden
was kind. Unkindness came from the rules,
which came from behind desert mountains.
I didn't say goodbye to my kids.
We were watching a soccer game when it happened.
My boyhood team is in a city that was steeped
in shipping slaves, water under the bridge.
Two of the goal scorers were Muslim.
One Senegalese, the other a Turk
who would have us believe
he's German. I forgot to say goodbye to the kids.
I sobbed, shook, woke up
with a dry face and a cloven heart,
uttered the Arabic word for it.
There's a world out there, people
no less beautiful than you are.
I lay down for an hour,
less water with time, recalled
the moment I no longer let my father touch me:
no more his little boy, his tenderness
wouldn't visit me the same again.
I felt his acceptance
unaware he'd begun waiting for mine.
It was after lunch, on the couch,
he stroked my hair, neck,

and forearm. It felt good then I felt older. Slowly,
I got up, walked away, his fingers trailing the air
of my wake, both of us wordless.
I didn't say goodbye to my kids.
There's a world out there, people
who don't ask me what I'm about
to say. You're not time.
I served with time and you're not it.

Syzygy

When I tell it, the first time I saw hail,
I tell him it was in a desert, knocked

a man getting out of his car unconscious
then drove a woman into my arms

because she thought the end was near,
but I assured her it wasn't so.

When he tells it, the first winter
after their hijrah was the coldest. Rare snow

came down, and his mother,
who knew what the fluff was

but until then had never seen it,
woke him and said, look outside, what do you see?

She called his name twice. He rubbed his eyes,
didn't reply. She said, this is flour from heaven.

When he tells it, he's an old man smiling
back to his mother.

Unacknowledged Pollinators

"If you were a star," you said, "you'd be called *Forgive me*."
To which I smiled (you couldn't see me) and said,
"Or *Forgive me not*."

You said "Beware the ides of March on days we're distant
from bees and flowers."

"Not if the bees in the mouth don't sting," I said,
"and the air we move is a monk's in a meditative year."

"Are we the plants or the particles,
the planets or the elements," you asked,
"and our touchless touching, vector-dependent sex,

and the honey mouth, are they the silences that waggle
the tune on our foraging routes?"

"When I say *honey*," I clarified,
"I'm asking you whose pollen you contain.
We're no snowflake symmetry

yet to each pollen grain its aperture:
porous, colpate, blanketing the earth
as crystals might, and light isn't refused."

"And when I say *honey*," you said, "you grip my sweetness
on your life, stigma and anthophile,

and the soporific folded on its synchronous river
that doesn't intend to dissect my paradise."

I said "Captive my captive, we lost and what did love gain.
I haven't fallen from where I haven't been
or exited what I didn't enter."

"Seen or unseen," you said, "you'll live in my mouth.
I have an extra room. The children like it there,

mead in it their stories and playdough."
"As if a child is the cosmic dust that made me,
and I'm the suffix, its -ide."

"And within that child a child."
"And within that another."

Solstice

It's always someone's birthday.
A school of mullets

rides the crest
of a wave like lizards

high on a dynamic
wall. Gust slices

through clouds blowing candles
waist-deep in water.

More seagull than pelican,
we gave up meat

for a year. Bread pudding
is our favorite desert.

Descending, Rising

It wasn't you inside your carrier that I loved
        (you needed new sneakers, daily steps of health).
I drew your image out to its source
        (it was lovely to have Niçoise salad by the sea).
The beaches were empty, the weather perfect
        (you said olive oil reserves the right to the shore).
We wed stars to beget an alphabet
        (from bodies to souls, and souls to corpses).
You said, the dead don't want to be brought back
        (I said I don't want to live forever alone).
In our backyard the jasmine won't let go of the rosebush
        (but can do without the thorns).
Half-stranger, which is your better half?
        (I describe you well and you veil me miracle).
Like the back of my hand, your heart
        (like the back of my heart, your hand).
I drooled on your jaw: you weren't repulsed
        (my pillow was dry: you sucked on my chin).
Memory cast a vote in our intuition
        (a consolation prize, no cancellation fee).
Some nights, from space, we saw Earth with the lit spots unlit
        (we did make hell a better place).
And wrote for future echoes each now becomes
        (within one made of zeroes and a zero made of ones).
With light debris in our genome, we talked
        (about what? the water level rose).
You said, the building blocks can't quit themselves
        (I said, our lives are a form their lives take).
                To gestate in delta
                (to gestate in delta).

Oxygen

Because to pin the moment I bound
with your blood, and your being

started to tick and flicker—I wasn't your first,
       and you weren't mine. Several

catastrophes preceded us, before I was the one
who could stay longest inside you

as you recoiled under pressure
and kicked out my gasp.

      Sometimes I rise above you blue.
      Between ignition and smothering

      we made a life of it,
      had each other
      opening to opening.

Carbon Copies

1-

Cattle in the agriculture of a self
besieged by the deceit of payback,

insurance against extinction,
there are other ways.

Everything in moderation.
The middle path comes after violence. No point

in whose brutality was on first,
who balked, and who walked it home.

2-

When we decipher memory
we'll have created another memory,

what kind of yearning and what response.
Longing and reflex are forever
in the package insert.

3-

You're a tourist in your identity.
From earthworms to diatoms,
extraordinary exhibition of ordinary

you behind love lines,
all the way behind them.

4-

You weren't parachuted in.
You were born in—back against the wall,

you screamed at grizzlies
but they were stuffed animals.

You sent us emails, holograms, online petitions:
"Maybe this, too, is love,"

you said, and they heard us
think it: neo-Cupids who asked us

"to find out how others love
differently than we love."

5-

Inert and bloated with DNA,
"All bodies are local," I shouted.

Another softly shot back, "Our bodies
are endless but we are all one."

That's when my wife shook me.
"For real, Fady, this is for real," she said.

Cancer

She glides her lily then lets him gild it,
he gilds his lily then lets her glide it,
the meadow's patient,
refractory

it waits, doesn't burst with flowers
shortly after
it has burst with flowers.
The earth depolarizes

the air that must do with light
what light does with ear.

You wanted too much,
she tells him, in and out
of serotonin's throes.

I wanted to grow a cortex, he says,
to better hear you with.

Blue Shift

Nightly, a longing, no repression
some trigger released,
snatches me, after the passing
of many years, *for who,*
I haven't a clue, the beloved
nameless beyond erasure,
when among the unsleeping,
a recrudescence
for the longing
to die better.

A longing behind a longing:
my illness is past
a certain ecstasy
in the thrill of betrayal, *nightly*
a life lived in disremembering
an interiority that *walks me*
far in search of one
whose end I write
in my calligraphy,
a stranger's end
nightly snatches me.

Not enough that she suffered
in headlines while so many
of our good hearts
refuse to believe
that they refuse
to believe, *names*
I count and remove,
or is this the suppression

you intend:
someone you know
is on the brink
of suicide, of murder,
is it also not
a national question?

If my love's eyes are stone
memory will
carve them still.
To die better,
I search my distances
for Fadwa and Alyssa,

they're doing well,
thank you for asking.
A consolation
that doesn't outlive hope,
a fatal disease we've made curable
mostly here, *and nightly*
longing exiles longing.

Nightly, your strings ring
me with friends
who go on singing
the hours, smoking the air,
drinking unaware
that I was
from among them taken.
And the names,
all but one, disappear,
if one's ever
lucky in our century.

Calligraphy for a Sagittarius

1.

Daily I think of you. Work
pours on my head (as people fall

off their lands and out with them).
Work and dogged bodies
that declare themselves

medicinal. Hospice is a dollar sign.
Pandemics are a long view.
And my recent exhaustion

is because a woman, colleague of mine,
suffered a pregnancy
that forced her off her feet.

The schedule has a hole the size of labor.
A placenta invades the uterus.

2.

Placenta, "blueberries
in leather casing," I say,
and you say, "a burnt out sunflower

in the sanguine heat of the womb."
Our conversation pauses for weeks.

Your blood pressure rises with the uprising
in the streets of a country
you can't call yours or want to—

we're children in parallel play:
I'm here, and over there
the unrest has no dog in your fighting years.

3.

This numberless numbering of a life,
your life, unforgettably forgettable.
When again we speak,

it's of your Arabic and of Arabic itself.
Allen was a wolf who howled to a saint

then informed one, we agree,
and was the wolf
who shared a meal with Farazdeq

across fire and smoke in Iraq
thirteen centuries ago
and counting. He might as well

have been Chief Guipago
of the Kiowa plains.

4.

Resurrection is our coma in orbit,
or coma in orbit is our resurrection:
near the sun we sublime.

As if graves are a masquerade,
our words are a greenhouse gas
we circulate. Alive

with Latin, for example, we refuse
to let a language die.

5.

I, too, spoke Arabic once,
learned love in it, which led me
to find love

in the English others see as theirs.
This is what I meant by listening:

how couldn't it be
that a thousand times
my voice walked by you blind.

Your Arabic
is beautiful,
so sing.

Mausoleum for a Scorpio

"Speak to us of poetry and politics,"
he said to me from his seat in the audience
as I was on stage. Throughout the weekend,
before the prize was made public, he was euphoric,
buoyant, generous, said his father was a tyrant.
"Say something about exile," he requested
a little later. We were in a small town
no one lives in, that patrons had turned
into a hostel for arts and culture, outpost
for fair and festival, colony for a future
that spares ranches, hiking trails,
vulture flocks that trim carcasses
and claim fences. The main hall was a restored
cottage where an icon was born: her mother
tended the land, her father walked to work
and home, and her brother, unaided,
built the treehouse in a pecan
we can still see. Later, the poet,
with mic in hand, took the stage and said
that he stood for beautiful things in literature,
for kind speech, then read a poem by a brilliant
woman who'd recently died. Troubadours aside,
he added, and pound for pound, the precious
lunacy of translation, "There's no language
like ours." We have Shakespeare, have abolished
consanguinity, erected a sky to bark up
the cellulose of time, "and I don't say this
to be bellicose," he preempted the thought
reserved for presidents, not prophets.
Far from morose in an age of infidels,

between his thumb and index, he held a daffodil
he'd plucked from a nearby pond, an anthem
he never abandoned. At dinner
he told me three decades had passed
since he'd come across a love poem a famous
Arab had written. He didn't like it. That's
alright, I thought, it's sentimental, rhymes
in the original, and its best parts
are untranslatable. He spoke with the tender
transparency of fibers liberated
from ill will. "And that Nobel Laureate,
he's great, but arrogant," he clarified,
"though another cried at the sight
of a hill in the backwoods of Burgundy."
"Shakespeare is not English," I said,
my poker face on. "You mean
he belongs to the world?" he replied
after a brief pause—then picked up a thread
from an earlier chat, on the mysticism
that pervades Asian shores,
occasionally setting sail
to us, or we to it: "As for the Sufis,"
he said, "it's all been done before."
And I hadn't taken him for a believer
in antecedence. Though it is
in his spirit that pigeons fly
as lightly as they alight.

Equinox

A gift economy stuffs its pockets
with stones that hold
       their shape like water.

We're more water than blood,
and more than water, a sea
       isn't a river, just ask the rain.

We're other worms
for other silk roads,

       a theory unified,
       a dream of nucleotides.

Isomers & Isotopes

1.

Our paradise is trampled.
Our childhood wasn't insured,
it endured in damaged dwellings.

1.

No paradise is untrampled,
it formicates us junkies.

We spin to love,
murder, suicide, and our lips
are our hips, silage and cud.

1.

As grownups, for decades
in pecuniary bliss,
our resale value tripled that of our parents.

2.

From room to room
the rain had risen from the sea,
from room to room our cells merged their fires
with the darkness of our sleep.

2.

The beat follows you affectless.

2.

The rain had risen from the sea to gentrify us,
Oh Aspergillus fumigatus, the detritus
was mostly next door.

2.

We met our deductible
and it was low.

We rolled our years
then smoked our years.

3.

I was a visitor,
was just visiting when she died
in the hospital where I was born.

3.

I was visiting her faculties as a plastic tube
sealed her windpipes which a mass
from her esophagus had burrowed into.

3.

In farewell she wrote on clipboard
"Revolution 'til we triumph."

4.

She went through a lot to get here,
through concrete and dried up in it.

Then pirates took her in. She learned their songs
and the earliest of them was in a wedding.

4.

"Ma'am, your fat pads are not who they say they are,
and since the rise of the eye-snatchers
we can't be sure of your retinal Hancock."

4.

I drabbled and droned semantic remorse,
Eddie the monster, Eddie the horse,
and was just at another queen's court

when my parents crossed as time on a rock
that pokes a rib chronic.

4.

"Ma'am, the shaman who offered you
the first stems to sprout in snow,
did she say her name?"

5.

In stereo, in stereo
we prolong the music,
we're good at rotating

light, polarizing it,
there's language between us.

5.

And clusters discrete from other clusters
to prevent our closing up on ourselves
as we wait for the sun to change its ways.

5.

Reliably the weather
invariably comes
with maps.

6.

If white came first, if red
stole the brain's flow until stars appeared
portals for blue.

6.

Omnipresent
the beast follows you affectless.

6.

Smooth gray hairless scalp
of a head preserved in rotting,
casing vestigial
and orbital cavities.

6.

The torso displays
arachnoid limbs and pterosauroid wings.

The splendor's in the thing's fluidity:
it flows in water and you walk on air.

6.

This isn't Death but the God
of your childhood enuresis.

Decades have passed
since you last wet your bed,
still your body insists
on messengers on mute.

7.

Dreams like phantom limbs.
Dreams of bladders on the verge.

7.

Therefore, the villages
are tickled with irrigation
and krill travels deep in a gray whale suit.

Therefore, herrings pleat coves
white with egg and sperm.

7.

As for sirens—those always cease when they reach me.
Those I always hear.

Aquarius

For eight years her parents tried
and couldn't conceive. A bedouin woman
passing through spoke her prescription: "Sacrifice
a white chicken together
on a moonless night, around
no artificial light, then go to bed."

An overwhelming majority
of the chickens were brown.
The entire quarter searched and found,
and nine months later the girl came out fair
"like her father," said the women. "No,"
the daughter says, "my complexion
I got from the chicken."

Elegy for a Kaleidoscope

We found her in Socorro etched on a tombstone
in a cemetery that's changed public and private boots and tarsals,
and grateful to the music of frontiers, between ebb and flow,
we made her ours. That her life split

the tail and head of two centuries, this we considered
relevant to our current standing in an expanding globe
and went on a search: a docudrama whose stack
of letters turned podcast for the cochleae of small towns,
lonesome households on terrains through a train's window.

This Southwestern find is Arab. A poet
without obituary, dug up on microfilm, an immigrant wife
whose husband's life, until now, was the one well archived.
They had two sons, no daughters, and our poet's best friend
was the wife of a missionary, first dean of a college

founded in Cairo. We adapted into film the letters the two wives
had exchanged. Records showed that her elder son was a falafel king
in Chicago then a shawarma po'boy fusionist in NOLA.
His daughter, a lawyer, litigated and won against Detroit's negligence
of its workers, and in Los Angeles, she married a Black entrepreneur,

but it hurt them when her uncle lobbied Congress that he was,
as Jesus was, Caucasian for citizenship. By then, our poet, our fulcrum
was gone: in her Cairene mail she'd left us a few poems.
Her verse offered English little. The few good lines that endure
spoke the usual wisdom in expired form:

The spirit is a magus irregularly good. God
is a fly you can't swat. A mosquito that doesn't need your blood
to go on living, still it settles on your skin.
And specks of the universe when we touch
the universe we touch ourselves.

Capricorn

To stand without eyes I wanted a tree.
With it came a city

> inspector: Is it a native
> species, she asked, a fire-hazard,

foundation-safe, roof-friendly, and why two
crabapples? she added. I want them

to have each other, I said,
besides, I'm not ready to learn from just one.

The inspector nodded
as she gazed up at the powerlines:
Trees see light, wave crests,

but no color, she said,
issued her permit and left.

> And where the two trees
> will stand I stood
> in their pose and closed my eyes.

House of Mercury

The storm funneled through town with destructive intent.
Fractured tree limbs, toppled fences, ripped shingles
like tufts of hair. Dad woke up to snaps and creaks,
the two live oaks in the front yard,
but in the backyard the nearly uprooted fig tree
brought him to tears. In the morning
two neighbors, one Black, one White
came over to bandage the oaks after debridement.
A third, an Indian, stabilized the fig tree,
pitched it like a tent with rope and stake.
On the second day, I cut up the rest of the branches,
deepened the earth for the fig, enjoyed a long lazy
lunch with my parents, and on the way home heard
a radio report on whether the sky is bluer
during a pandemic. The third day
I took my son and daughter back,
we bundled up the heaps, nursed the flower beds,
delighted in another languid lunch,
hummus, falafel, shakshuka
followed by tea and stories about fear
that comes to nothing. The kids said it was the best falafel
they'd ever had. And Mom said that going forward
her morning glories will get the light they deserve.

Postcard from a Virgo

All your tides and rhythms buoyant
like that water bird from the bayou,
the lone gray heron you're used to spotting
at night in your neighborhood streets,
when the season's right,
bathed in yellow light. Is it possible
the bird is blue? The gray species has a shorter life,
and you've been telling me about those feathers
for a decade. A doppelgänger, perhaps,
in on the retreat within your
retirement ropes. The seasons that may not be
what they've been for us
answer their roll call in orbit. In my city we swap
eco for eros and toads come bubbling.
My lifespan doesn't clarify my consciousness.
And my revolution is in hours.
Between a sunflower's florets and the galaxy,
cellular and solar, I am outgrown.

Gemini

After yoga, I took my car to the shop.
Coils, spark plugs, computer chips, and a two-mile walk
home, our fossilized public transportation, elementary
school recess hour, kids whirling joy, the all-familiar
neighborhood. And then another newly demolished house.
How long since I've been out walking? A message appeared
on my phone: an American literary magazine
calling for a special issue on Jerusalem, deadline approaching,
art and the ashes of light. At the construction site
the live oak that appeared my age when I became a father
was now being dismembered. The machinery and its men:
almost always men, poor or cheap labor, colored
with American dreams. The permit to snuff the tree
was legally obtained. The new house is likely destined
for a nice couple with children. Their children
won't know there was a tree. I paused to watch
the live oak brutalized limb by limb until its trunk stood
hanged, and the wind couldn't bear the place:
who loves the smell of fresh sap in the morning,
the waft of SOS the tree's been sending
to other trees? How many feathers will relocate
since nearby can absorb the birds?
Farewell for days on end. They were digging a hole
around the tree's base to uproot and chop it
then repurpose its life.

Domicile, House, Cusp

If my last hope is reached, I'll have reached my last fear,
we'll have landed our homelessness at its terminal variant.

           *

Our promise of value is the regime of it.

And describing you
        is an immersion in nine alphabets during conquest.

But finding another rock that circumambulates you and settling it
        is like waiting for Mecca.

           *

Can you see me? Anatomically speaking, I speak from the left,
        and handling panhandled my speech.

Can I touch you? A space was available.
        And what doesn't dwell in the abode it's in?

           *

        My mourning
is an animal and my animal a constellation.
        My gratitude
goes to the doctor who complied with my demands.

           *

Half-stranger, your devotion to patina marks me:
fossil fanatic, sediment digger, covetous

     of what doesn't break
     or alter under duress
     on the road of being a return to you,
     and the road is the world.

*

Your son, she said, will eat each olive you pick
then plant each pit in a circle around the tree.

     "So that his eyes are the light the dead give life to,
     and his hands are in the earth."

*

To lose sight of lost sight
     I turn my hearing into proprioceptive cadence:

my first encounter with a me I've not met in person.

*

Scarred as a sea that's ceded a rocky shore
to the claws of elements, I hold up my spine,
bifurcate breath in pressure
sacs for keeping alive.

*

You're not a language I am
　　　　ashamed to sing. You're a language I'm not
ashamed to sing. Does life know bigger fans than us?

　　　　　　　*

Sometimes illness is a labor union, and science, capital.
Illness rubbed me gravely once and I didn't care for visitors.
　　　　I spit blood. It passed.
　　　　I loved them back.

　　　　　　　*

We're ready to go where we're not ready to be,
　　　　a mask falls off another mask
'til there's none to don: we manufacture more.

　　　　　　　*

Black vulture, black vulture,
there are no nursing homes in your heart,
no vocal cords in your throat.
Thousands of years passed.

Along the way I deciphered echo,
things you had said to me
as I dunked my head in water.

　　　　　　　*

　　　　Thousands for an archipelago of organs.
　　　　For a truce with the self invisible to others.
　　　　An internal sky choked with clouds.

*

Your language, she said, is land,
but your land is not a nation. And your sea,
she said, is the appendix to God's speech,
so what preposition does your echo take?

*

Directional echo to inconsequential reply, I'd be ignorant to deny
the ubiquitous reverb, a feverish swirl to examine
the patience I pour over loss.

*

A patience you've nurtured well,
an albedo you can't sink our enamel in.

*

A desert mirage, a province for all none can claim
to themselves alone, and our friendship across a hundred
and one faces.

*

We wheeze, wheeze
with constricting, cartilaginous rings.

We're asthma, and larger than a cohort
of motes a light beam stirs.

*

We wanted something to galvanize
            our frog legs and defend the title
of the organism around which,
            around which.

*

I descended to embalm rapture.

*

Litigious not lentiginous,
you pulled a mackerel out of a bucket.

Someone's dying, you said,
but in a newborn, language is ready to occur.

*

            More air conducts me to you than me to me.
            More bone conducts me to me than me to you.

            Air is the distance. Bone is the difference.
            And a nuance in the sand is Daedalus.

*

In the house that houses our darlings.

A chair for a voice, a desk for the wind.

Aries

Duhkha: a vanishing of suffering, an Odyssey
that rams me into Sisyphus, Ithaca's other name.

Duhkha: I don't pronounce it properly
or insert the proper symbol for it in Word doc,
a dot at the mouth of the cove the first h makes.

Duhkha sounds like the word for laugh in Arabic,
the noun not the command and in dialect of dialect
duhkha imagines duqqa:

herbaceous, nutty, spiceful,
pounded into coarse powder that adheres to bread
you dip in olive oil every morning. Or dizziness:

when you see duhkha laid out on the page
you can hear the Arabic for dizziness. For falafel,

couscous and sumac combined,
and humus is mine.

Three Leaps of the Gazelle

"O serene self, returnee to God,
you're fulfilled and contented

to enter his creatures and paradise."
"If a hope isn't misplaced

just a little, it's no hope at all."
"And the space between raindrops a shelter."

"The mountaintop a lake."
"The gecko an oriole."

"The athel a bulbul."
"And I'm seagrass and you the banyan."

Black Hole

Of impermanence, on whose
edges the last escape is infinite,
if it is death this destiny
offers me, and in its tail end
a conduit to another realm
in which time spins differently
than we've known it to pass:
a purpose that heaven and hell
served for as long as they could
before they ran out of gas
with no wormhole out of God
to show for. An extinguished
imagination masquerades
as exchangeable commodity.
Sometimes a pit grows
a supermassive mouth,
can swallow its children
but doesn't.

Libra

Before a bear mauls me,
before I slam
into the ground from a height I had
no business reaching,
before a bullet

bleeds me apparitional,
and before drowning
after surviving the fire
of a plane I did not board
until it was in midflight,

first I was alone
then with loved ones
who disappeared unharmed.
It's rare to witness oneirically another's
death, beloved or not,

even if the roads are populated
with posts, and the dead,
when they reappear,
are always alive.

I'm not blind. I hear nothing
during my rapids, though they are
like a doughnut, speech-filled
with letters I decrypt
after I wake. Their dots
mark my mind

with the day's senses
as poetry is to a dictionary.
Is there a gauge
for joy in the reel of sleep,
is there dancing before bed?

Through nightmare, I can't
stay calm, can't trust that
whatever ending may come
will not be my end: and if mine,

who am I to deflect it from my body,
untagged, temporary corpse,
paralyzed so that I
don't harm myself
in the psychosis of wanting

to save myself or others
from neurotransmitters
depleting, replenishing
in contact zones, the noble
civil war of sleep.

Yes there is joy:
now and then
a chase frees me of gravity,
the hunt terminates,
and the air
turns viscid beneath my feet, a high

so physical that I'm not done
rising and gliding
like a ballerina
in my still waking:

it takes me
a minute to suspend my belief
in my superpower, my will
to stay alive
is autonomic.

And my will
to fall back asleep.

The Old Lady and the House

Forty years ago, Lucy bought the land, split the lot, built two houses, sold one, lived in the other. Ten years ago, we moved in next door. For months we only saw Paul, her husband, faithfully out for a smoke on the front lawn, with Sue, their playful gray shih tzu in tow. "She loved the previous owners' kids," was his welcoming remark, her poop across our lot. Our son was one-year old. Paul was about to enter his seventies, and Lucy, a good few years older, was fitter, more vigorous, but neither walked their Sue. Paul watched the chronicles of the neighborhood, a paradisiac Bantustan, our little city of god. A year earlier Fatima and I visited San Miguel de Allende to restore our minds in eco-friendly destinations. She was five months pregnant. We were living in an apartment complex that a hurricane would drench after toppling its papier-mâché chimney. In San Miguel, the Gringo-run B&B was a fairytale structure straight out of the palaces in Sentra. Half-owner, the local wife cooked us Christmas dinner, denounced the natives who "like being poor," as her husband radiated his traumatized Californian youth through a book's help that scored all religions to a barometer of Zen. Islam scored lowest. Paul was a veteran with an enlarged prostate. His advice was that I should "watch out for them" who blow my fallen live oak leaves, they're bound by law to dispose of the waste "free of charge," leave none of the black plastic bags on my curb, an eyesore for other residents. A month later, I asked Jesus (leader of the landscapers who'd come to the U.S. as a child during the Zapatista Revolution) to trim the live oak branches, including those that straddled the corners of the two backyards. But "Issa," as Fatima liked to call him, (*Jesus's* pronunciation in Arabic) remonstrated that as dogs and fire hydrants are as good as apple pie, he wouldn't cut a single branch that covered a parallax of that man's yard. "Your neighbor, he's, how you say it," as he stuttered a rhyme with a cystic illness attributed to Ra, the ancient sun god. I corrected Jesus's pronunciation. Paul's health began to change. Lumbago herniated his golf swing. He quit smoking. The body that nicotine once infused turned diffuse. His abdomen, rotund. He contracted diabetes. Soon there was no more small talk, no navy stories. I'd find Paul outside, his shoulders closed toward a street I couldn't call him back from. Dementia and hospitalization started their record of his life. Lucy struggled with the decision to put him away in a nursing home. "I remarried a younger man so that he'd take care of me when I'm older," she was bothered, "and I hate fat people," she added with a shiver as she bearhugged herself. Thin throughout her life, always in proper robe when outside her door, and if intercepted with a greeting, she'd quickly apologize for her hair and the Texas sky, though I'd never seen her or Paul out to Church on Sunday. Paul was now well cushioned into his dying. When he stopped recognizing her, she stopped visiting him. Then daily she watered her yard and plants, and weekly she mowed her grass, a sloth born a bee in a solo hive. One afternoon she knocked at my door, her voice trembling, and I let her in. She said her landline was out of commission, that she'd just been released from the hospital for hypertension, a minor stroke after a fibrillation. I plugged her phone back into the wall and thought her end was near. Our niceties atrophied. She was the tea-drop-stained figure in a photo rarely pulled out of a box. She no longer heard my car come up the driveway, my doors slam open and shut, my half-hearted hellos. That was five years ago and yet: when she and I had hardly exchanged a word for months, and she'd run into my mom in our driveway, Lucy, unprompted, would praise me. A testament to her classy decorum, thoughtful of another mother's heart. Then rain fell anthropogenic. And all the houses on our street left us hydrophobic of a swollen firmament. When water receded, everyone on the street walked out to talk with each other, nouveaux ions in calamity's bonds. Lucy's only son came to her rescue and cut to the chase: a woman of 90 can't live unassisted in a house under repair. The property would be fixed then sold, he declared, but Lucy wouldn't sanction the sale, and a few months later moved back in. During remodeling, the rubble lined her front lawn and swamped the crape myrtle that stood on the border between us. On the heap a burgundy leather shoe bulged like a boat. It was Paul's right edematous foot before he was packed out. The second time I came across the shoe I looked for its other half. What would I have done with it had I found it? Lucy's still living in her house. First alone then in incremental hours with a caregiver. Lucy asks her not to come back and is frustrated when she does.

Altair

Then a grackle being a grackle
landed on the hood of your car,
you behind the wheel, engine off

in Home Depot's parking lot
(you'd bought a commode
lid and a toilet flapper with chain
after the flood). A bird doesn't need

much vocabulary, mostly the best
of the live oak acorns
in the gully, the cowl.

Event Horizon

Stars hang on a rim,
their pulsating

shudder's an echinoderm
growing back its limbs

in the abyssal depths,
a bioluminescence

of the departed.
Stars telegram me:

if I'm reproducible,
I'm not necessarily

an inheritance.

Sirius

Don't event blink. Let streams
behind your lids slip into sea.
The sea as human in the human,
marine in the marine. Hear
only your breath
then your heart. Commit
what you can control
to stillness. The rest
was born as movement
in you before you were born
and shall remain
sensorial eternity
trapped in atmosphere.
Your brightest guide is a hound
who'll rescue you out of a circle
of guards. Be motionless
water, run in place or don't run.
You won't dry up, you're more
than starlight in ashes
or symbionts riding swells.
You're mostly
of this earth, and more cloud
than ground. There's
what drinks you for life.
You'll be everywhere.

Year of the Metal Dog

Plainspoken   the grass is grave.

You preferred the life you lived   overcame hunger
then satiety   pleasure then displeasure
that noble   kryptonite.

For years you'd been austere epiphanies, words of mouths that drink from
Lethe, but now in a field of poppies, the longest sentence arrives:

the dog's ecstatic astonishment that those who abandoned him would always
return, the apples and oranges on long hospital nights, the feet freed bare
on cool grass, and the shoes that led them there,

the first sip of water in the morning, the acid reflux washed down, squirrels
on a hickory, light breaking onto bark, and you emptying your bowels which
can hold for days what a camel hump can hold for a year.

You lived fully. Grew parsley, rosemary, and turnip. Purchased the rest of your
produce on Tuesdays from a street market after the coolest imitation of fire.

You were an urn on top of a pillar in a temple carved in hematite. A whole
language against a pair of lips. You swam with seal and duck. Got high, got
drunk, shredded carrots, juiced the lemons, crushed the garlic, and on occasion

told the unjust they too will die, and thus can take a piss before bedtime, and
on occasion you were unjust.

You rejected the passport, accepted the vaccination and the microbiome, and
under a brilliant sky, refined your glands, counted florets on a dandelion.

And on your birthdays you sang and danced with children.
As on their birthdays they sang and danced with you.

&

Venus Cycle

Was I ever a moth
or you this kind of light?

One of us was dying, and one
had no wings for the journey back.

My heart   which has been wrong
more times than I can count

                                  has been right more.

It tells me what yours tells me   there will be trouble,
                                  confusion, but no war.

And no heart catheterization will alleviate

                                  the blocked roads to you,
yes, but this: of two in distance always one is

the more severed.   The episode lives
its natural course: we're not wounds, not whole.

Walking in a forest we hear white thunder.
But no white thunder lives in this forest.
We had not walked in this forest before, and the trees,
redwoods, are not trees we live with,
they're trees we visit. A redwood has decided to surrender
one of its dead. The rumbling rotten limb kills you
or me, and life is changed for those who grieve us.

We go out for a second cigarette
on the balcony during a lull in the war.
I feel that I will have you
forever because I have lost you for good.
You say the sea jazz in the morning sends
a briny breeze to your pores,
and away from the sea you're insomniac.
The sea in you is a fever. No one does well
when they don't sleep well,
it's literally torture.
And the world doesn't care
because all hearts are in love.
What I left behind to love you,
and what you, me.

What if I walked my rhythm to yours,
listened to my body as you listen to your body?
And when you're not listening well
I can listen to what in you taught me listening.
We can't bleed together
but we can breathe together.
So that when I'm a stranger in the world
I can find you.

To kiss you again,
your soft eyes,
the hermeneutics of your
hospitable highway
to my chattering wheels.
I shut my mouth,
pave a road for you, a country
road stripped by ranch

and meadow hum.
I was looking up at you,
rolling joints with your nipples,
and all you said was "I'm so wet,"
as if God had commanded me to read,
to trace the lace,
and you curled fetal,
let me spoon you, let my hand
drain the blood from your head
as behind your lids
you travelled into why
after why an orphean kiss is fine:
I want to be hurt
to dissipate into plumage
for seven years in which you're not
sound or sight.
I'd like to kiss you
then to the Gulag go missing.
Where your cheek meets your neck,
my nose leads my lips.

It is the rhythm of distance.
If the rhythm of my distances
from you is as yours from me.
Or maybe the distances
we offer others are our asking
for the distances we'd like to receive.
Neither postulate is true alone.
A nameless desire is tamed when named,
and spring lasts longer than its bloom.
We're living a staggering carnival
with aloe minarets, cacti cupolas,

the paloverde mothering the fence,
honeysuckle's jasmine envy,
and a thorny metamorphosis,
a jellyfish gone terrestrial with
diaphanous red petals,
anthers like a chandelier
of crisp fried crumbs
on a sushi roll. I enter
already assimilated.
The thought that distracts from
the experience of the body
is an experience of the body.
That stalk we watched rise above all
others in the garden of a mystery packet
you bought last summer opened
its satellite face for days,
astrolabe of our hearts—foreign,
novel, thrilling, it was
the distance thrower we flamed.
This close, this alive, this haptic
on my phone screen,
your "good morning" to me
for weeks. We identified the flower
on a search engine.
It was common.

Every hour, sixty memories.
What's for dinner?
Who'll pick up the kids from school?
Lunch boxes.
Soccer practice.
Either pleasure

gives in to this line of questioning
or rules supreme over click-and-send.
Eros unto dying.
A randomized open-label
for two horses trading necks
between ecstasy and the monks
of falling into themselves.
Worms have no I,
they have you and me.

And home has a home in the heart.
In your textile skin, ambling dermatomes,
trabeculations of my heart,
in air or water, little stones
sculpt sound:
systole folds what diastole opens,
big bang, the inaugural heart.

And the moon wanes to crescent
then grows back its heart.
My root, your root
come home to root:

a life is wasted
that did not love,
so how can we perish?

Can you hear
our balance stones
bathing in the waves,
diaphragms slipping and sliding?

Your shoulders dive
away from your auricular pools.
My breath asks for less

eavesdropping.
Is your heart expanding?
Are there any statues

left standing
in mine? The feeling
images our brains:

a dove at our window
with a sealed note in its beak.
A dove at our feet.

A pigeon. A cooing
silhouette tagged for sitting
at the edge of taste.

The water was clear.
We stayed in it.

Acknowledgment & Notes

Several poems here appeared first in earlier versions in the following publications: *A Poetry Congeries; Arc Poetry Magazine; Free Verse Online; Hyperallergic; Image Journal; International Poetry Review; Kenyon Review; Michigan Quarterly Review; Mizna; New York Times Magazine; On the Seawall; Plume Poetry; Poets.org; Rusted Radishes; Subtropics; Under a Green Warm Linden; Yale Review; The Baffler; The Nation; The Spectacle.*

"The Holy Embraces the Holy": the title is a tribute to Amjad Nasser (1955-2019)—a phrase from his brilliant meditation on place in his long poem *Petra: The Concealed Rose*. The description of historians as "camp followers" is from Inga Clendennin's essay, "'Fierce and Unnatural Cruelty': Cortés and the Conquest of Mexico": Historians are the camp followers of the imperialists."

"Blue Shift": the italics are adaptations of lyrics from a song in Arabic by Fairuz: أنا عندي حنين.

"Three Leaps of the Gazelle": the title comes from an asterism in Ursa Major established in Arabic astronomy. The first quote in the poem is an adaptation of a well-known verse in the Quran.

Cybele Knowles

FADY JOUDAH has published four collections of poems: *The Earth in the Attic*; *Alight*; *Textu*, a book-long sequence of short poems whose meter is based on cellphone character count; and, most recently, *Footnotes in the Order of Disappearance*. He has translated several collections of poetry from the Arabic and is the co-editor and co-founder of the Etel Adnan Poetry Prize. He was a winner of the Yale Series of Younger Poets competition in 2007 and has received a PEN award, a Banipal/Times Literary Supplement prize from the UK, the Griffin Poetry Prize, and a Guggenheim Fellowship. He lives in Houston, with his wife and kids, where he practices internal medicine.

milkweed
editions

Founded as a nonprofit organization in 1980, Milkweed Editions
is an independent publisher. Our mission is to identify, nurture and
publish transformative literature, and build an engaged
community around it.

Milkweed Editions is based in Bdé Óta Othúŋwe (Minneapolis) within
Mní Sota Makhóčhe, the traditional homeland of the Dakhóta people.
Residing here since time immemorial, Dakhóta people still call Mní
Sota Makhóčhe home, with four federally recognized Dakhóta nations
and many more Dakhóta people residing in what is now the state of
Minnesota. Due to continued legacies of colonization, genocide, and forced
removal, generations of Dakhóta people remain disenfranchised from
their traditional homeland. Presently, Mní Sota Makhóčhe has become a
refuge and home for many Indigenous nations and peoples, including seven
federally recognized Ojibwe nations. We humbly encourage readers to
reflect upon the historical legacies held in the lands they occupy.

milkweed.org